OTTER NONSENSE

by Norton Juster   pictures by Eric Carle

Philomel Books
New York

Published in the United States of America by Philomel Books,
a division of The Putnam Publishing Group, 51 Madison Avenue
New York NY 10010. Published simultaneously in Canada by
General Publishing Co. Ltd., Toronto. Manufactured in the
United States of America.
Library of Congress Cataloging in Publication Data
Juster, Norton, 1929–
Otter nonsense.
1. Animals—Anecdotes, facetiae, satire,
etc. 2. Animals—Caricatures and cartoons.
3. Puns and punning. I. Carle, Eric.
II. Title.
PN6231.A5J87 1982   818′ .54′ 02   82–9821
ISBN 0-399-20932-8   AACR
ISBN 0-399-20931-X (pbk.)

For Emily who is udderly charming

Seal of approval

Oxidentally on porpoise

Lemming meringue pie

A precarious perch

An aardvark
and an even aarder vark
taking a vark

Raven mad and cocksure

An inchworm
jumping a foot
out in the yard

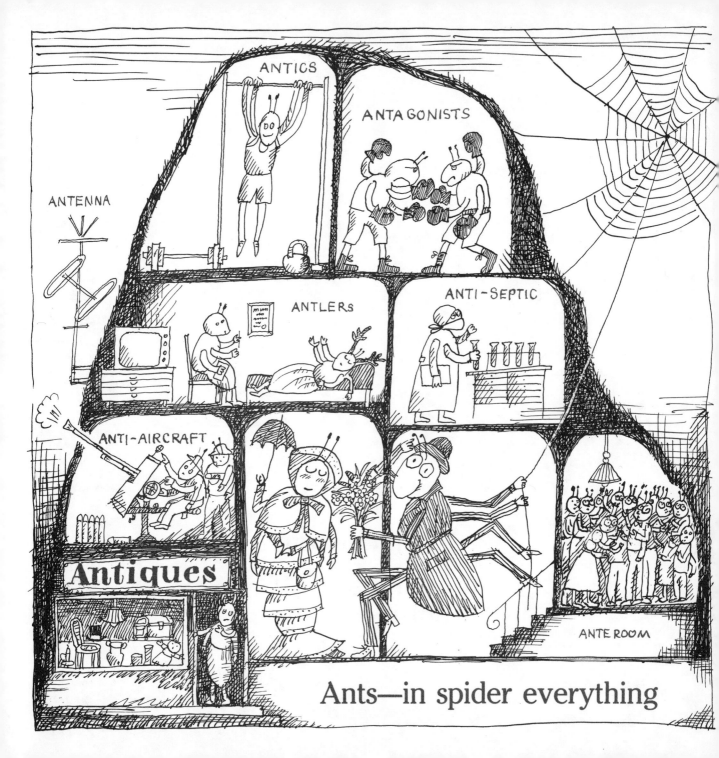

Ants—in spider everything

Hippocrit

Ambassador and ratify

Crocodull

Crocoduel

A moose with a mousetache

A mouse with a moosetache

A golf lynx
with cuff links

A pair of cheap skates   Fast buck

Chipmunk   Gopher broke   Terrible cheetah

Heron gone

Ram-page

Lamb-ent

Ewe-phoric

A dandy lion lyin' down

Roe, roe, roe your boat

All the gnus that's fit to print

A dugong and   a don't gong

A froggy day
in Londontown

Pups
Pupulation
Pupcorn
Soda pup
Pupsicle
Puppets

Dog tired

Terns

Out of tern

A tern for the worse

One good tern deserves another

Wrens

Wrendition

Wrenovate

Wrenegade

Larks and bagel

Shaking hens

Roofrus

Walrus

Floorus

Harecut

Asstronomer

Donkey Hoty

Bear up &
bear down

A locust and a highcust

Ballgame

Baseball bats

A bunting

Ferret out

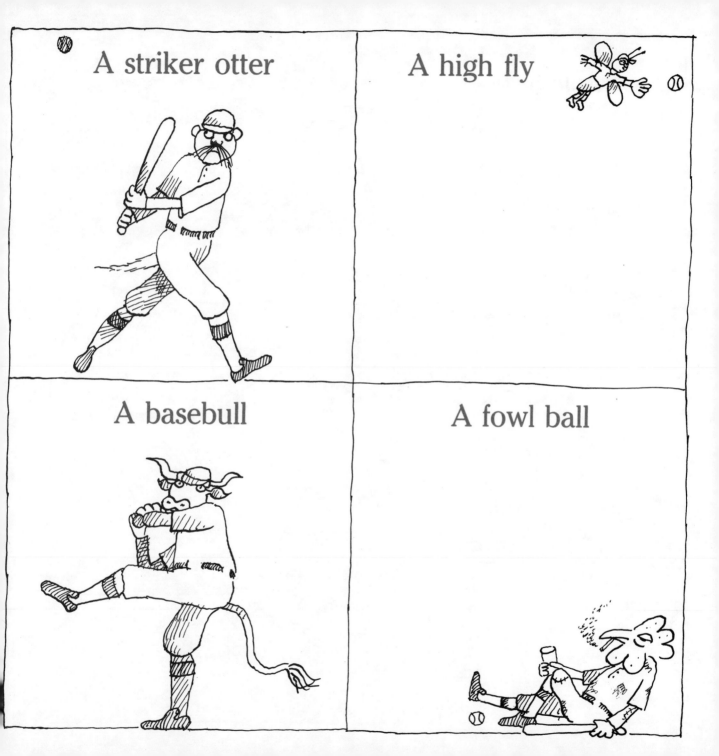

Mole-ar

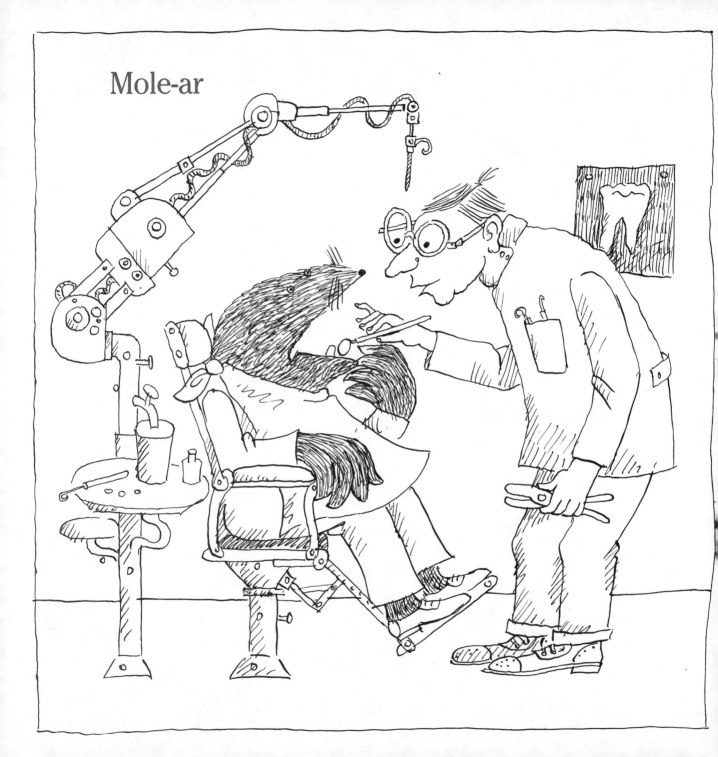

A hoarse horse horsing around in the horsepital, and Doctor Mallard E. Lingerzon (a real quack!)

Clam up

Weasel overcome and eagle opportunity

Bisontennial

Otter otters

A patriotter

An otter plotter

An otter potter

We hope you've had some fauna.

No newts is good newts.

Mug Shots

NORTON JUSTER, the author of this book, is an architect, professor of Environmental Design at Hampshire College and author of a number of children's books, including *The Phantom Tollbooth, The Dot and the Line* and *Alberic the Wise*. He lives with his wife and daughter in a small town in western Massachusetts.

ERIC CARLE, who drew the pictures in this book, is the creator of *The Very Hungry Caterpillar, The Honeybee and the Robber* and many other beautiful and beloved picture books. He is married, has a daughter and a son, and lives in an even smaller town in western Massachusetts.